lates

NEW HOLLAND

REAL FOOD FOR FAST PEOPLE

LYNDEY MILAN
photographs by Michael Cook

To my parents, Isabel and Bill Hall, who showed me the value of good home cooking and warm-hearted entertaining and to my children, Blair and Lucy, who carry on the tradition.

Published in Australia in 1999 by
New Holland Publishers (Australia) Pty Ltd
Sydney • Auckland • London • Cape Town
14 Aquatic Drive Frenchs Forest NSW 2086 Australia
218 Lake Road Northcote Auckland New Zealand
24 Nutford Place London W1H 6DQ United Kingdom
80 McKenzie Street Cape Town 8001 South Africa

First published in 1995 by William Heinemann Australia
(a part of Reed Books Australia); reprinted 1996
Reprinted 1997 by Hamlyn Australia (a part of Reed Books Australia)
Reprinted 1999 by New Holland (Australia) Pty Ltd

National Library of Australia Cataloguing-in-Publication Data:

Milan, Lyndey.
Plates: real food for fast people.

New ed.
Includes index.
ISBN 1 86436 484 X.

1. Quick and easy cookery. I. Title.

641.555

Publishing General Manager: Jane Hazell
Cover Design: Big Cat Design
Internal Design: Joanne Miller
Photographs: Michael Cook
Accessories: Accoutrement
Printer: L.Rex Printing Co. Ltd

The recipes and photographs first appeared in the *Sydney Weekly*.

CONTENTS

introduction   v

no plates!

POTATO ROESTI WITH SMOKED SALMON   2

OYSTERS WITH DIFFERENT TOPPINGS   4

THAI FISH CAKES (TOD MAN PLA)   6

SMOKED SALMON & NORI ROLLS   8

CHINESE DUCK ON RICE CRACKERS   10

STUFFED ZUCCHINI FLOWERS   12

HERBED OLIVE OIL WITH VEGETABLE BREAD   14

FIGS IN PROSCIUTTO   16

EASY SAN CHOY BAU   18

PORK DIM SIMS   20

MUFFALETTA   22

light plates

ARUGULA, PARMESAN CHEESE
& PROSCIUTTO SALAD   26

'SANDWICHES' OF EGGPLANT, VINE-RIPENED
TOMATO & GOAT'S CHEESE   28

SPRING VEGETABLE SALAD   30

CHAR-GRILLED VEGETABLES WITH OLIVE OIL   32

SMOKED SALMON CRÊPE CAKE   34

MUSHROOMS EN BRIOCHE   36

AROMATIC VEGETABLES   38

MICHAEL'S MUSHROOM RISOTTO   40

PENNE ALLA NAPOLITANA   41

SPICY THAI PRAWNS   42

PRAWNS & FENNEL IN GARLIC CREAM SAUCE   44

PRAWN & MANGO SALAD
WITH SWEET CHILLI SAUCE   46

SEAFOOD RAVIOLI   48

DEVILLED PRAWNS   50

CHINESE CHICKEN SALAD   52

ASIAN-SCENTED BROTH
WITH CHICKEN WONTONS   54

SPAGHETTI WITH PROSCIUTTO & ROCKET   56

SPIRELLI PASTA WITH CRAB & LEMON   58

FOCACCIA WITH LAMB & TOMATO SALSA   60

KANGAROO TAIL SOUP   62

large plates

HOKKIEN MEE NOODLES   66

MODERN SALAD NIÇOISE   68

FISH WITH CHERMOULA MARINADE
& COUSCOUS   70

TUNA WITH WASABI & FRESH HERB BUTTER   72

WHOLE THAI-STYLE STEAMED FISH
WITH CHILLI, GARLIC & CORIANDER 74

PASTA WITH PUMPKIN, HORSERADISH
& SILVERBEET 76

SPRING SALMON 78

THAI BEEF SALAD 79

PASTA WITH CHICKEN LIVERS, SAGE & ROCKET 80

CHICKEN BREASTS IN PROSCIUTTO 82

CHICKEN BREASTS
WITH RED CAPSICUM AÏOLI 84

GREEN CURRY OF CHICKEN 86

KANGAROO FILLET
WITH RED-CURRANT REDUCTION SAUCE 88

PAN-FRIED STEAK
WITH TOMATO & OLIVE SAUCE 90

LAMB STEAKS WITH ROASTED RED CAPSICUM
SAUCE AND COUSCOUS 92

LAMB MINI-ROAST
WITH GARLICKY WHITE BEAN PURÉE 94

BOURBON PORK WITH GLAZED APPLES 96

sweet plates

BAKED QUINCES WITH ALMOND TUILES 100

HONEYED FIGS 102

STICKY TOFFEE PUDDING 104

PLUM CLAFOUTIS 106

BREAD & BUTTER PUDDING 108

CRÈME BRÛLÉE 110

POACHED PEACHES WITH GRANITA 112

GRATINÉED FRUIT 114

RHUBARB & STRAWBERRY CRUMBLE 116

SUMMER PUDDING 118

LEMON OR LIME TART 120

YUMMY LEMON PUDDING 122

STONE-FRUIT TART 124

PEAR CONFIT 126

TINY PASSIONFRUIT BUTTER TARTS 128

HONEY WAFERS
WITH CHOCOLATE & MACADAMIA NUTS 130

basics

MAYONNAISE 134

MICROWAVE HOLLANDAISE SAUCE 134

PESTO 135

VINAIGRETTE 135

BEST-EVER SCONES 136

CRISPY FISH BATTER 136

SUGAR SYRUP 137

BASIC BEEF STOCK 137

index

138

INTRODUCTION

Food in Australia has changed markedly in my lifetime. Meat and three veg has given way to a myriad of exciting, different food styles and flavours from countries as varied as our multicultural population.

Yet good food is timeless. Never has it been so easy to create. We have the best produce in the world: fabulous ingredients, which are best treated simply, allowing the flavours to speak for themselves. So why are we losing our cooking skills as a nation? As we become more computer and technology literate, it seems we are becoming less food literate. We are becoming a nation of people frightened of real food.

plates : REAL FOOD FOR FAST PEOPLE seeks to redress this. Fast food is not necessarily junk food. At home we no longer have the time or inclination for tricky food. We want food that looks fab and tastes good, but is prepared in next to no time. This is the type of food that I love to cook and which has proved so popular in the pages of the *Sydney Weekly* and *Melbourne Weekly* and is now presented in this book. Here I must thank June McCallum, my first editor at the Weekly, for convincing me to do it; Chong, who has continued with warm-hearted support and Eric Beecher, who started it all. Yet none of this would have been possible without my colleague and friend, wonderful food photographer Michael Cook. Some of the recipes are his also.

Though recipes and definite amounts are given in this book, my whole philosophy is to cook by feel, look and taste and not be constrained by instructions. Use the recipes as your point of departure and inspiration. It is most important to cook for yourself and your loved ones the wonderful abundance that our country has to offer. Above all, teach the next generation to cook. It's easy and it's fun.

So happy cooking and – even better – happy eating.

no plates

POTATO ROESTI WITH SMOKED SALMON

Simple and stylish, this idea can be used as finger food with cocktails or as an entrée (as pictured). Either way it is delicious.

Peel, grate, rinse and drain some potatoes. Squeeze them dry, then fry in a large pan in round pastry cutters, pushing down with a potato masher or the back of a spoon to compress. When golden brown, turn over and fry on the other side until golden. These can be served warm or at room temperature, and can be made well in advance of serving.

To assemble, spread roesti with crème fraîche and top with a generous amount of good quality Tasmanian smoked salmon.

OYSTERS WITH DIFFERENT TOPPINGS

2 dozen oysters

freshly ground black pepper

juice of 1 lime

1 teaspoon Thai sweet chilli sauce

2 tablespoons tomato pasta sauce

2 shallots, sliced

1 tablespoon fresh ginger julienne

1 tablespoon sweet vinegar seasoning
or rice wine vinegar

1/2 teaspoon sesame oil

Top some of the oysters with freshly ground black pepper and lime juice. Top others with a mixture of Thai sweet chilli sauce and tomato pasta sauce. My favourite combination is a mix of shallots and fresh ginger julienne with Japanese sweet vinegar seasoning and sesame oil.

Oysters must be the most perfect food — and the easiest to serve as they require very little preparation.

Pictured are premium-grade Sydney rock oysters and Pacific oysters (the larger ones).

THAI FISH CAKES (TOD MAN PLA)

A dish that has quickly become a favourite and is really very easy to make. However, once made the fish cakes need to be eaten immediately. They do not reheat well, though if you use fresh fish you can freeze the mixture before cooking, but you do lose some liquid when it thaws out.

1 kg sweet lip, red fish fillets or similar

1–2 tablespoons red curry paste

100 g green beans, finely sliced

1 tablespoon kaffir lime leaves
(if dried, soak for 10 minutes then slice)

2 tablespoons finely chopped
coriander leaves and root

1 egg

2 teaspoons sugar

1/2 teaspoon salt

oil for frying

DIPPING SAUCE

1/2 cup (125 ml) vinegar

1 cup (250 g) sugar

1 teaspoon salt

3 tablespoons water

1 small onion, finely diced

1 small carrot, finely diced

1 medium-sized cucumber, finely diced

coriander leaves, chopped

chilli, optional

For the fish cakes, simply put all ingredients except the oil into a food processor and blend. Roll the mixture into balls in the palm of your hand, then flatten a little. Fry in oil until golden brown, then turn over and fry on the other side. Serve with sauce.

To make sauce, boil vinegar, sugar, salt and water for 1 minute. Pour over the remaining ingredients. Taste and add extra vinegar, sugar or salt if necessary.

Makes approximately 80 small fish cakes

SMOKED SALMON & NORI ROLLS

smoked salmon

1 tub hard
cream cheese

few drips sesame oil and/or
a little chopped dill

nori seaweed (optional)

Mix the dill or sesame oil (or both) through the cream cheese. Cut the salmon into rectangles (two or three from each slice, depending on size) and put a little of the cream cheese mixture into the middle of each piece. Tuck under the ends and roll to form a neat parcel. Cut seaweed in strips and soak briefly in water. Roll around the middle of each salmon roll.

These rolls will keep for a couple of days in the fridge or, if you really must, they can be frozen.

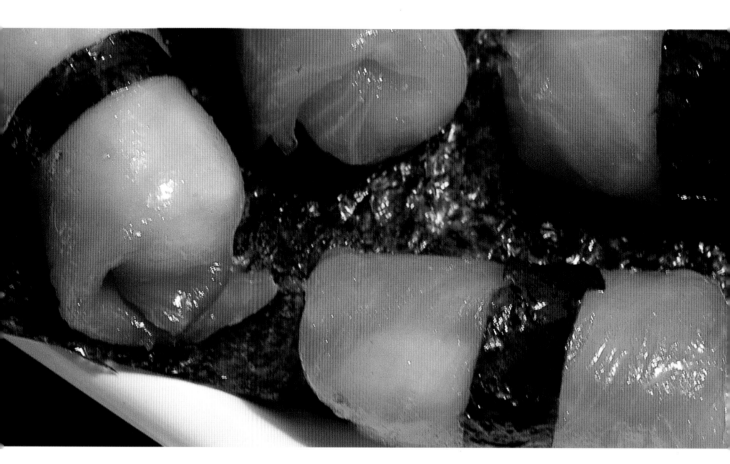

Smoked salmon is perennially popular. This is a more modern way of serving it, especially if you use the seaweed that can be purchased at Asian food stores.

CHINESE DUCK ON RICE CRACKERS

No cooking at all is needed for this dish. It is a little like Peking Duck finger food, so get ready to stand back and accept the compliments! Buy the duck from an Asian shop or even a Chinese restaurant. Ask for it not to be chopped.

$^1/_2$ or 1 whole Chinese barbecued duck

1 packet Chinese rice crackers

$^1/_2$ bunch shallots, finely sliced

hoi sin sauce

Remove the flesh and skin together from the rib cage and bones of the duck, preferably while it is still warm (because then it's easier). Slice into pieces to fit on rice crackers. It may be refrigerated at this stage until required.

When you are ready to serve, add a sprinkling of shallots and a dollop of hoi sin sauce – and you have one of the best canapés around!

1 packet of rice crackers makes 68 canapés

STUFFED ZUCCHINI FLOWERS

Zucchini flowers have become much more readily available, and they are delicious stuffed. I am always a little disappointed when they are simply battered and deep fried, as then all you can taste is oil and batter!

1 punnet zucchini flowers

STUFFING

1 slice thick white bread

1/4 (60 ml) cup milk

1/2 teaspoon salt

2/3 cup (125 g) ricotta cheese (or chèvre)

1/4 teaspoon chopped fresh oregano or
2 tablespoons chopped basil

1 clove garlic, crushed

1/4 cup (25 g) grated Parmesan cheese

1 egg yolk

ground pepper

BATTER

flour

beaten egg

breadcrumbs, cornmeal or beer batter
(see p. 136)

oil for frying

Soak bread in milk and, when soft, squeeze dry. Mix all stuffing ingredients together, adding some milk if the mixture is too stiff.

Spoon or pipe the stuffing into the zucchini flowers. Then steam the flowers or dip in flour, beaten egg and breadcrumbs, cornmeal or beer batter and fry.

HERBED OLIVE OIL WITH VEGETABLE BREAD

No real recipe for this one, just some ingredients and the ultimate taste test!

extra-virgin olive oil	freshly ground black pepper
freshly chopped herbs, e.g. basil, chervil, dill, parsley	lemon juice
salt	small loaf of multi-coloured vegetable bread, sliced

Use your very favourite extra-virgin olive oil, stir through a generous handful of freshly chopped herbs and season to taste with a little salt, pepper and lemon juice.

Serve in a bowl as finger food, surrounded by slices of colourful vegetable bread. Keep a spoon on the serving tray so that you can stir the oil before each dip, to keep the herbs from sinking to the bottom. This keeps very well in the fridge, and just needs to be brought back to room temperature for serving.

FIGS IN PROSCIUTTO

So simple you do not really require a recipe! It relies on the beautiful flavour of figs in season. The quantities will depend on the size of the figs, so you'll have to estimate.

fresh figs   prosciutto

Cut the fresh figs into eighths if they are large. Remove the rind from the prosciutto and cut each slice into three or four pieces, they should be large enough to wrap around a fig segment.

A longtime favourite in my household. My kids call it 'Chinese hamburger'.

crisp iceberg lettuce

2 tablespoons oil

750 g lean pork mince

1 small cup water chestnuts, drained and chopped

4 slices fresh ginger, peeled and chopped

1/4 cup (60 ml) chilli sauce

2 tablespoons dry sherry

1 tablespoon soy sauce

1 teaspoon sugar

salt and pepper to taste

2 tablespoons cornflour

1/2 cup (125 ml) chicken or beef stock

Carefully separate lettuce leaves and trim with scissors to form neat cups.

Heat a wok or fry pan and add the oil. Stir-fry the pork, chestnuts and ginger in the oil until the meat is no longer pink. Stir in the chilli sauce, sherry, soy sauce, sugar, salt and pepper.

Blend the cornflour and stock together and add this mixture to the wok or pan. Cook for a further 1–2 minutes, stirring.

Place the cupped lettuce leaves on a serving plate and fill each leaf with 3–4 tablespoons of the warm stir-fried mixture. Roll up the leaves and serve.

Serves 4

PORK DIM SIMS

50 g bamboo shoots, drained

3 shallots or
1 medium onion, sliced

1 bunch garlic chives,
chopped (optional)

500 g finely minced lean pork

1 packet wonton wrappers

SEASONING

2 teaspoons soy sauce

2 teaspoons dry sherry

1 teaspoon salt

2 teaspoons sugar

$1/4$ teaspoon black pepper

2 teaspoons sesame oil

1 tablespoon cornflour

I came up with this recipe when looking for something to cook for Chinese New Year. Traditionally, these dim sims would be deep-fried after steaming but, ever mindful of the needless addition of fat, I prefer to serve them steamed. The flavour is better too!

Finely dice the bamboo shoots, shallots and garlic chives (if you are using them) in a food processor. Add pork and blend until smooth. Add seasoning ingredients and mix well.

Place a generous spoonful of this mixture in the centre of each wonton wrapper and pull up the sides to make dumplings, the pastry should nearly reach the top of each one.

Arrange the dim sims in large greased bamboo steaming baskets and steam over high heat, covered, for 7–8 minutes.

Simply serve direct from the steamer with a little bowl of sweet chilli sauce.

Makes 25–30 dim sims

MUFFALETTA

Knock the socks off your friends when you take this to your next picnic!

1 large Italian-style white loaf	marinated mushrooms
olive oil	mortadella
prosciutto	artichoke halves
provolone (or any other cheese you like)	sun-dried tomatoes
sliced, fried eggplant	salami
roasted red capsicum	olives

Take the loaf of bread, slice it in half horizontally and remove a little of the soft bread. Brush the insides with a little olive oil. Layer the ingredients in any combination and order you like. Put the top back on the bread. Wrap in foil and weight down for several hours before eating. If you pack the loaf at the bottom of the esky with everything else on top, it will be perfect by picnic time. Cut into wedges or slices and serve.

light plates

ARUGULA, PARMESAN CHEESE & PROSCIUTTO SALAD

1 red capsicum	Parmesan cheese
1 French stick	goat's cheese
1 bunch arugula or rocket	olive oil or butter
6–8 slices prosciutto	balsamic vinegar

First, roast a red capsicum in the oven, or over the gas burner or barbecue until it is black and blistered. This takes around 20 minutes in the oven. Place immediately in a plastic bag and leave until it is cool enough to handle. This makes it easier to peel. Remove the skin and seeds and slice into strips. While the oven is on, slice some French bread into rounds, brush with olive oil or butter and place in the oven until crisp and dry.

Wash and dry a bunch or so of arugula. Grill some slices of prosciutto. Grate some fresh Parmesan cheese or, better still, slice with a peeler. Spread some goat's cheese over the French bread croutons and place in the oven.

To assemble the salad, cover a large platter or fill a bowl with the arugula, sprinkle on top the crisp prosciutto, Parmesan cheese slices and the roasted red capsicum strips. Garnish with goat's cheese croutons. Drizzle the olive oil and balsamic vinegar over the top or use your favourite vinaigrette (or the recipe on page 135), sit back and enjoy the compliments and the salad!

Serves 4 (or more or less!)

Again, more a food idea than a recipe. Follow your head and use quantities that suit you, expanding or contracting them to match the number of diners. Arugula is now freely available in any of the better fruit and vegie markets. It is sometimes called rucola or rocket. It has a spicy, peppery taste. If you can't get it, use watercress instead.

'SANDWICHES' OF EGGPLANT, VINE-RIPENED TOMATO & GOAT'S CHEESE

1 red capsicum	3 vine-ripened tomatoes
2 evenly shaped, long eggplants	250 g goat's cheese
salt	pesto (optional)
olive oil	basil leaves

Roast the red capsicum in a hot oven, or over a gas burner or barbecue until it is black and blistered. This takes around 20 minutes in the oven. Place immediately in a plastic bag and leave until it is cool enough to handle.

Slice the eggplants thickly. You will need twelve slices. Sprinkle with salt and leave in a colander for an hour or so. Wipe dry and cook in hot olive oil until brown on both sides. Drain on absorbent kitchen towel.

Slice the tomatoes and goat's cheese thickly. You will need six slices of each. The aim is that the rounds of eggplant, tomato and goat's cheese are roughly the same size.

Place half of the rounds of eggplant on a baking tray. Top with a slice of tomato, a slice of goat's cheese and finally another round of eggplant. Bake at 200°C for 10 minutes.

Skin, seed and slice the capsicum.

Place the 'sandwiches' on serving plates and top with pesto. Garnish with basil leaves and strips of red capsicum.

Serves 6

It is interesting to see how spontaneous food ideas seem to spring up simultaneously in different places. There are many versions of these 'sandwiches'; I particularly like this one.

A delicious salad, which can be adapted to suit seasonal vegetables at any time of the year. With it is a terrific shallot mayonnaise that comes from chef Gillian Hirst at Il Centro Restaurant in Brisbane. Don't be daunted by the list of ingredients and the different steps. It is not difficult, the flavours are wonderful and the shallot mayonnaise can be used in many other ways.

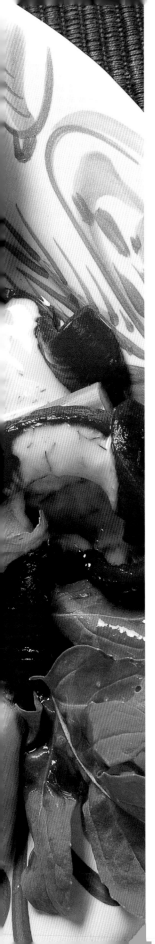

SPRING VEGETABLE SALAD

SHALLOT MAYONNAISE

1 chopped green shallot

1 tablespoon herbs,
e.g. parsley, chervil,
dill, basil

1 soft-boiled egg

1 teaspoon
Dijon mustard

juice of 1/2–1 lemon

1/2 cup (125 ml) olive oil
(or to taste)

salt

pepper

SALAD

8 spears asparagus

4 medium pink-eye (also known as
southern gold) or desirée potatoes

1 large red capsicum

1 medium purple onion, thinly sliced

2 whole artichokes or an equivalent
quantity of good quality preserved ones
(the best are usually found in jars)

4 dessertspoons shallot dressing

virgin olive oil

arugula or rocket lettuce

freshly ground black pepper

To make the mayonnaise, chop the shallot and herbs in the food processor. Add the egg, mustard and lemon juice and blend until smooth. Slowly add the olive oil with the processor running. Season with salt and pepper.

Simmer the potatoes in lightly salted water until just cooked, leaving the skin on. Blanch the asparagus spears in lightly salted boiling water, then refresh them in iced water. Roast the capsicum in a very hot oven until the skin blisters, then place in a plastic bag. When cool enough to handle, peel away the skin, and clean out the seeds. Slice into 1 cm slices, reserving liquid from inside the capsicum. Strain if necessary. Assemble the salad on four plates, starting with the potatoes, halved, in the centre. Place a quarter of the sliced onion on the top of each, the artichoke half to one side and the asparagus spears over the salad. Arrange the capsicum where it looks most striking and put a spoonful of dressing on the potato. Drizzle a little virgin olive oil over the salad and divide the capsicum juices between the plates. Garnish with the arugula and freshly ground black pepper.

Serves 4

CHAR-GRILLED VEGETABLES WITH OLIVE OIL

eggplant	oyster mushrooms
kumara	light olive oil
onion	extra-virgin olive oil
zucchini	sea salt
capsicum	black pepper

Preheat your barbecue or a heavy pan with grill markings, such as a Le Creuset. Slice the vegetables, they need to be cut up carefully to keep pieces as flat as possible for cooking this way. Leave the oyster mushrooms whole. Brush sliced vegetables or, better still, spray them with light olive oil and place on the grill. After a couple of minutes, lift them up and turn them around 90°, so that they cook with a cross marking. Repeat on the other side.

Serve with good-quality, extra-virgin olive oil, sea salt and black pepper.

We have a great variety of vegetables in this country and some of the best are often overlooked. Cook them in this way and even the most fussy eater will ask for more. Use any vegetables you like, but I suggest you choose them in different colours so that the dish is very colourful.

SMOKED SALMON CRÊPE CAKE

For a festive touch, make these champagne crêpes.

CRÊPES

5 eggs

1 tablespoon sugar

1¹/₄ cups (325 ml) champagne or sparkling wine

2 tablespoons (30 g) butter, melted

1 cup (150 g) flour

salt

2 tablespoons (30 g) butter for cooking

FILLING

1 tablespoon chopped dill

1 carton crème fraîche or sour cream

20 thin slices smoked salmon or trout

Blend eggs, sugar, champagne, butter, flour and a pinch of salt. Rest for half to one hour. Melt butter for cooking in a crêpe pan and add enough mixture for one crêpe, cooking until it is dry on the top. Turn it over and cook the other side. This side should be golden. Repeat until all crêpes are cooked. Mix dill with crème fraîche and spread some on a crêpe, top with two slices of smoked salmon, then place another crêpe on top and continue in this way until the stack is finished. Cover in plastic wrap and chill.

To serve, cut straight through the layers like slicing a cake.

Serves 6 or more

MUSHROOMS EN BRIOCHE

A basic recipe for a mushroom ragout that can be served in a little pot or ramekin with crusty bread, used as a sauce on any meat or pasta for a main course or served en brioche as a stylish entrée.

Buy individual brioche from your patisserie, allowing one per person. For the ragout, select a variety of fresh mushrooms; preferably at least three of the following: shiitake, field, Swiss brown, enoki, abalone or oyster, cup or button.

1 kg mixed mushrooms
butter
$2/_5$ cup (100 ml) beef stock or wine

$1^1/_4$ cups (300 ml) thickened cream
salt and freshly ground black pepper
8 individual brioche

Wipe the mushrooms clean with some paper towelling or a soft cloth. Slice the larger mushrooms, leaving the small mushrooms whole for variety. Sauté them in butter in a frypan. Stir in a little beef stock or wine, cream, season with salt and pepper and bring to the boil, simmering until it is reduced and slightly thickened.

Meanwhile, remove the bump on top of the brioche and scoop out a little of the filling. Place them in the oven to warm while the ragout thickens.

Remove brioche from oven. Spoon some of the filling into each brioche, allowing it to spill over the edge onto the plate. Replace the lid.

Serves 8

AROMATIC VEGETABLES

The ideal accompaniment to any dish or simply to enjoy on its own.

3 medium carrots, cubed

3 medium zucchini, cubed

3/4 cup (250 g) peas

20 snow peas, sliced

2/5 cup (100 ml) cream

250 g butter

extra butter for sautéing

1 small leek, sliced

1 dessertspoon each of
chopped thyme, chives, basil, chervil
and tarragon

salt

Blanch the vegetables (except the leek) in boiling water and refresh under cold water. Set aside. Reduce the cream until it is just thick. Whisk in the butter. Set aside.

Heat a little butter in a pan. Lightly sauté the leek and then the blanched vegetables. Reduce the heat and add the cream/butter sauce. Sprinkle generously with chopped herbs. Season to taste and serve immediately.

Serves 4, 6 as a side dish

MICHAEL'S MUSHROOM RISOTTO

A recipe from Michael Cook, the photographer. I can't believe that something so simple and that goes against all the accepted rules could taste so good! I find any pungent dried mushrooms, such as boletus or cèpes, work equally well.

1 cup (200 g) arborio rice

3 cups (750 ml) water

10–20 g coarsely crumbled dried porcini mushrooms

olive oil

salt and pepper

1–1¹/₂ teaspoons Vegon vegetable extract

freshly grated Parmesan cheese

Simply place everything except the Parmesan cheese in a microwave-safe container with a firmly fitting lid. Cook on HIGH for 10 minutes. Stir, then cook on HIGH for a further 10 minutes. Remove from the microwave, there should still be some liquid left. Allow to stand 5 minutes or so to complete the cooking and absorb the liquid. Add another good slosh of olive oil (or butter to be more traditional), mix through and serve with freshly grated Parmesan cheese.

Serves 3 people (it would serve more but it's so delicious it rarely does in my house!)

PENNE ALLA NAPOLITANA

Another simple recipe from intrepid photographer and foodie, Michael Cook.

salt	3–4 garlic cloves
olive oil	1 large can of good quality Italian tomatoes
150 g penne pasta	basil
extra-virgin olive oil	Parmesan cheese

Put plenty of water in a pot to boil with a little salt and oil, to prevent the pasta sticking together. Put the penne in when it is at a rolling boil.

At the same time, in another pan put a good slosh of extra-virgin olive oil and crush some garlic cloves into it when hot. Cook until the garlic is fragrant and brown, then add the can of tomatoes. Bring to the boil and reduce to a simmer. Stir occasionally. When the pasta is ready, so is the sauce. Drain the pasta, toss through the sauce, adding some basil if you will, and freshly grated Parmesan cheese. Enjoy immediately.

Serves 2

SPICY THAI PRAWNS

Thai food is based on a balance of hot, sweet, sour and salty. These flavour components can be adjusted according to taste.

1 tablespoon oil

1–3 fresh red or green chillies to taste

2 onions, chopped

6 tablespoons chopped garlic

1 tablespoon minced ginger (optional)

2 tablespoons chopped coriander root
(from one bunch of coriander)

400 g shelled green prawns

1/2 bunch shallots, finely chopped

2 tablespoons sugar

1 teaspoon salt

4 tablespoons lemon juice

4 tablespoons fish sauce (nam pla)

chopped fresh coriander

Heat oil in pan or wok and sauté the chillies, onions, garlic, ginger and coriander root until the onion is transparent but not brown. Add prawns and shallots and continue to cook until prawns are opaque and almost cooked. Sprinkle over sugar and salt, then add lemon juice and fish sauce. Taste and adjust the spiciness with chillies, sweetness with sugar, sourness with lemon juice and saltiness with salt or fish sauce.

Serve with the coriander sprinkled over the top.

Serves 4

PRAWNS & FENNEL IN GARLIC CREAM SAUCE

2 tablespoons butter

1 large onion, chopped

$^1/_2$ bulb fennel, finely sliced

4 large cloves garlic, minced

400 g shelled
green prawns

salt and pepper

$^4/_5$ cup (200 ml) cream

Melt butter in a frypan. Sauté the onion and fennel until tender, then add the garlic. Add prawns to pan and stir until they are opaque. Add salt and pepper to taste, then the cream. Bring to the boil, reduce a little and serve immediately.

Serves 4

I developed this recipe when teaching a class at the Sydney Seafood School. I wanted to demonstrate that the same ingredient (in this case, prawns) when handled in different ways went with entirely different wines. So this recipe is suited to a chardonnay, the Spicy Thai Prawns to an aromatic riesling, while prawns in a salad with asparagus go well with a sauvignon blanc. Try it for yourself!

PRAWN & MANGO SALAD WITH SWEET CHILLI SAUCE

The idea for this recipe came from my colleague Peter Meier, who is from Casuarina in the Hunter Valley and a long-time lover of Asian flavours.

DRESSING

¹/₂ bunch shallots,
chopped including some of the green part

2 teaspoons chopped ginger

1 tablespoon chopped lemongrass
or 1 tablespoon lemon zest

1 tablespoon Thai sweet
chilli sauce

2 tablespoons fresh lime juice

2 tablespoons vegetable oil

1 tablespoon chopped coriander

1 large mango, ripe but firm, diced

20 shelled and deveined green king prawns

few sprigs coriander for garnish

Place all the dressing ingredients in a jar and shake well to combine. Divide mango among serving dishes and spoon over just a little of the dressing. Poach prawns briefly in boiling salted water. Do not overcook them. Drain and, while still warm, toss in the remainder of the dressing. Place five prawns on each plate, top with the remaining dressing and garnish with a sprig of coriander. Alternatively, all the ingredients can be combined in a large bowl. Serve hot or cold.

Serves 4

SEAFOOD RAVIOLI

I love this recipe. Seafood ravioli are so terribly glamorous yet, using wonton skins, so easy to create. They have a silky texture, just like good hand-made pasta. You will need to allow at least two ravioli per person and each ravioli takes two wonton skins.

1 cup (250 ml) fish stock

³/₅ cup (150 ml) cream

splash of white wine (optional)

1 packet wonton skins

little milk

selection of seafood, such as 1 prawn, 1 scallop and 1 small cube of fish per ravioli

chopped fresh herbs

To make the sauce, reduce the fish stock, cream and wine (if you are using it) until thickened. Lay out wonton skins on a flat surface. Paint the edges with a little milk using a pastry brush or your finger. Place your selection of seafood, I suggest a prawn, a scallop and some fish on top of each wonton skin. Cover with another wonton skin and squeeze together around the circumference to join. Cook briefly in salted boiling water. Add chopped fresh herbs to the sauce. Place the individual servings of ravioli in bowls and top with the sauce. Eat and enjoy!

DEVILLED PRAWNS

3 tablespoons oil

1 onion, sliced

1 green chilli, sliced

2 cloves garlic, chopped

3 slices fresh ginger

1/4 teaspoon turmeric

1 tablespoon paprika

1 teaspoon chilli powder

1/2 teaspoon chilli pieces

2 pieces lemongrass

4 or 5 curry leaves (optional)

12 shelled and deveined
green prawns

lemon juice and salt to taste

Heat oil in a pan. Add all ingredients except the prawns, lemon juice and salt, and stir. Then add the prawns. Toss briefly until cooked. Add lemon juice and salt and serve immediately.

Serves 2–3

This recipe was popular when demonstrated on television by Asian foodie Felicia Sorenson when she visited Sydney.

CHINESE CHICKEN SALAD

2 chicken breasts

Cajun spice mix

2 tablespoons
mayonnaise

2 tablespoons
sweet chilli sauce

cashews

1 small can of mangoes, diced

lettuce

interesting bread,
such as capsicum, olive, etc.

CAJUN SPICE MIX

1/2 teaspoon onion powder

1/4 teaspoon garlic powder

1/2 teaspoon ground oregano

1/4 teaspoon ground nutmeg

4 teaspoons sweet paprika

1/2 teaspoon cayenne pepper

1/2 teaspoon caster sugar

1/2 teaspoon black pepper

1/2 teaspoon turmeric

1/2 teaspoon salt

Dip the chicken breasts in the Cajun spices. Alternatively, just use a mixture of paprika and black pepper.

Grill, cool and chop into small cubes. Combine the chicken with mayonnaise, chilli sauce, cashews and mango. Serve by placing lettuce on the bread and topping with the chicken mixture.

Serves 4

This recipe is thanks to David Turner, chef at Sheraton Towers, Southgate, Melbourne. If you are not able to buy a Cajun spice mix, try mine, which accompanies the recipe.

Another deceptively simple dish to create, yet it looks and tastes sensational.

ASIAN-SCENTED BROTH WITH CHICKEN WONTONS

4 cups (1 litre) chicken stock or consommé

2 teaspoons Ketjap Manis
(Indonesian sweet soy sauce)

2 tablespoons mirin

2 large shallots cut into 3-cm pieces

1/2 fresh chilli

1 stalk coriander (optional)

1 chicken breast

salt

12 wonton skins

1 tablespoon milk

1 cup (250 ml) extra stock
or salted water

coriander leaves and chilli for garnish

Combine the stock, Ketjap Manis, mirin and shallots in a saucepan and bring to the boil. Meanwhile combine the chilli, coriander (if you like it), chicken breast and salt in the food processor and process until well mixed. You can leave it with a coarse texture or process to a smooth paste.

Bring the extra stock or water to the boil.

Lay the wonton skins flat and brush the edges with milk. Place 1/2 teaspoon of the mixture in the centre of each skin. Fold over and press together with your fingers to form a neat semi-circle.

Drop each wonton into the simmering stock or water and cook until they float. They cook very quickly, in a matter of moments. Don't cook them in the chicken soup as it will turn cloudy. Remove the wontons and place in bowls. Top them with the simmering soup. Garnish with coriander leaves and, perhaps, some fine slices of chilli.

Serves 6

SPAGHETTI WITH PROSCIUTTO & ROCKET

spaghetti or fine other pasta

2 slices prosciutto about 2 cm wide

extra-virgin olive oil

2 cloves garlic, crushed

1 bunch rocket or arugula

Parmesan cheese, freshly shaved

Cook the spaghetti or fine pasta in plenty of salted, boiling water in the usual way. Meanwhile, dice the prosciutto.

In another pan, warm some olive oil, add a crushed clove or two of garlic and toss it around with the prosciutto. When the pasta is done, drain it, toss it into the pan with the prosciutto and garlic. Add some leaves of rocket and serve immediately with fresh Parmesan cheese. The heat in the pasta will gently wilt the rocket.

Serves 3–4

The ultimate fast and easy recipe; this is based on a delicious pasta dish I had recently in Rome. There smoked marlin was used. I have substituted prosciutto. Ask your deli to slice some prosciutto thickly for you.

SPIRELLI WITH CRAB & LEMON

Use spirelli or spiral pasta for this dish as the sauce clings to it beautifully. Fresh crab meat is sometimes available from your fishmonger, so order it to save having to cook a crab yourself.

150 g spirelli pasta
(around 75 g of raw pasta per person)

1¼ cups (300 ml) pure cream

zest of 1 lemon

100 g fresh crab meat

salt and pepper

Cook the pasta in plenty of salted, boiling water. When it is almost cooked, simply heat the cream with the zest of a lemon. Then stir in the crab meat, return to the boil and season with salt and pepper. Serve immediately over the hot, drained pasta. If you prefer to use less cream, replace some of it with fish stock.

Serves 2

FOCACCIA WITH LAMB & TOMATO SALSA

2 onions

olive oil

1 large focaccia or
4 small round focaccia per person

8 lamb steaks

pesto (optional) (see p. 135)

(see p. 135)

TOMATO SALSA

3 tomatoes, finely diced

1 Spanish onion, finely diced

$1/2$ bunch basil,
freshly chopped

salt and pepper

Sauté the onions in a little olive oil or cook on the barbecue hotplate.

Make the salsa by combining the tomatoes, onion, basil and salt and pepper.

Cut focaccia in half horizontally and place on the grill, with the outside next to the heat. Char-grill or barbecue the lamb steaks, turning quickly to prevent overcooking.

When the focaccia crusts are crisp, remove them from the heat. Spread the bottom half with the pesto (if you like), then the onions, trim lamb steaks and tomato salsa. Close with the other half of focaccia.

Serves 4

In warmer weather this is ideal for the barbecue or indoor char-grill. Alternatively, the normal grill is fine. What's important is that this is a fast, easy, fun and hassle-free dish.

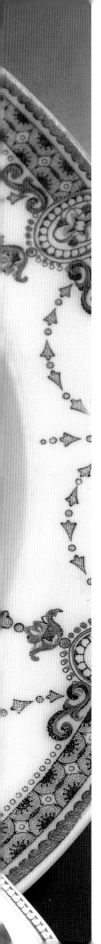

KANGAROO TAIL SOUP

The idea for this recipe comes from my colleague Barbara Lowery, cookbook author and ABC food broadcaster.

2 tablespoons (50 g) butter

1kg kangaroo tail

1 large onion, diced,

2 medium carrots, diced

1 stick celery, diced

8 cups (2 litres) beef stock

1 bouquet garni
(sprig fresh thyme, parsley stalks)

fresh ginger cut into julienne strips

fresh coriander

Melt half the butter and brown the kangaroo tail, then transfer the meat to a plate. Add the remaining butter to the pan and cook the prepared vegetables gently until lightly coloured. Add the stock, kangaroo tail and bouquet garni. Bring to the boil and simmer soup for 2–3 hours, skimming occasionally. If the simmer is very gentle and you skim carefully, there is no need to chill the soup to remove the surface fat, though this is an alternative.

Then add a julienne of fresh ginger and some fresh coriander leaves to the soup and serve. If you prefer not to have bones, you can take the meat off the bones.

Serves 6

large plates

HOKKIEN MEE NOODLES

1 packet fresh Hokkien mee noodles

vegetable oil

1 teaspoon sesame oil

4 chicken thigh or 2 chicken breast fillets

1/2 bunch shallots, chopped

2 red chillies, deseeded and finely chopped

2 tablespoons freshly grated ginger

1/2 bunch fresh coriander

4 tablespoons Ketjap Manis
(Indonesian sweet soy sauce)

Simply sauté the sliced chicken fillet – breast or thigh (the thigh is more flavoursome and moist) – in a pan, preferably flavoured with a little sesame oil. Add the chopped shallots, chilli (use capsicum for colour if you don't like chilli) and grated ginger.

Heat the noodles in boiling water and toss through the chicken mixture. Stir in some freshly chopped coriander and Ketjap Manis.

Serves 4

Hokkien mee noodles are available in all Asian food stores. They are wonderfully thick, round noodles. One theory has it that Marco Polo took the concept of noodles from China to Italy, where they developed into pasta! One packet should feed four.

MODERN SALAD NIÇOISE

If you never liked traditional Salad Niçoise with tinned tuna, try this with fabulous fresh ingredients and you will soon change your mind.

500 g fresh tuna

olive oil

mixed lettuce

500 g baby new potatoes,
boiled, peeled and sliced

1 punnet cherry tomatoes

1/2 cup black olives

3 hardboiled eggs, sliced

1 small tin of anchovies (optional)

350 g beans, blanched and sliced

DRESSING

6 tablespoons olive oil

2 tablespoons wine vinegar

salt and pepper

1 teaspoon French mustard

2 tablespoons chopped fresh herbs

Place tuna in a dish that fits it snugly. Cover with olive oil and cook in the oven at 150°C for 20–30 minutes, until just done. Cool in the oil. Remove from the oil, drain and slice into chunks.

Layer lettuce, potatoes, cherry tomatoes, olives, eggs, anchovies, beans and tuna in a dish.

Combine the dressing ingredients in a jar and shake vigorously. Pour over the salad and serve.

Serves 4

I was lucky enough to go to Morocco with the International Olive Oil Council in 1994, and I picked up some wonderful food ideas there. Chermoula is a traditional Moroccan marinade or sauce.

FISH WITH CHERMOULA MARINADE & COUSCOUS

6 pieces firm fish such as ling

lemon wedges

MARINADE

juice and grated rind of 1 lemon

1 teaspoon ground cumin

1 teaspoon ground coriander

2 teaspoons sweet paprika

3 tablespoons olive oil

2 tablespoons chopped parsley

2 tablespoons chopped coriander

pinch of salt

COUSCOUS

180 g instant couscous

1/2 cup (125 ml) stock

2 tablespoons mixed dried fruits

2 red chillies

2 tablespoons toasted pine nuts

2 tablespoons chopped coriander

salt

pepper

Combine the marinade ingredients in a food processor. Place the fish in a shallow dish and pour marinade over it. Cover and, if possible, let the fish marinate for 2 hours in the fridge.

Place the fish under a pre-heated grill, basting it with the extra marinade while grilling. If there is any remaining marinade, heat it and serve as a sauce with the fish and lemon wedges.

To prepare the couscous, pour the stock or water over the couscous and leave it to swell.

Pour a little boiling water over the dried fruit to plump them up. Seed and finely chop the chillies. Combine the couscous, chillies, dried fruit, pine nuts, coriander, salt and pepper. Heat in a pan with a little olive oil, stirring frequently, or in the microwave.

Serves 6

Each family has its own, usually secret, recipe. Couscous is the perfect accompaniment to this fish dish, but it would also complement many other recipes in this book.

TUNA WITH WASABI & FRESH HERB BUTTER

1 clove garlic

1 tablespoon chopped fresh coriander

2 tablespoons other chopped fresh herbs
of your choice, such as dill or chives

2 tablespoons prepared wasabi
paste or powder

2 teaspoons Dijon mustard

2 teaspoons soy sauce

freshly ground black pepper

250 g butter, softened

olive oil

4 thick tuna steaks

salad mix

balsamic vinegar

olive oil

Mince the garlic in the food processor with the herbs. Then add the wasabi, mustard, soy sauce, pepper and butter and blend. Turn out on a piece of greaseproof paper, foil or plastic wrap and form into a fat sausage. Freeze or refrigerate to harden until it is required.

Heat a pan with a little olive oil. When it is very hot, put the tuna steaks in it, brown them on one side and then turn them over. The aim is to have the fish brown and crispy on the outside and pink on the inside. Serve immediately topped with a slice of the wasabi butter and some salad mix from your greengrocer, over which a little balsamic vinegar and good olive oil has been drizzled.

You will find that this recipe makes more than enough butter for four tuna steaks, so I suggest that you freeze about half of the butter – it will be great for an impromptu meal.

Serves 4

Fish frightens many home cooks, but cooked simply and quickly it is delicious, stylish and, above all, fast and easy. The quality of tuna and our markets is always superb, as it must be to be suitable for eating raw as sashimi. This dish unites tuna sashimi with soy sauce and wasabi on its head for a dense, unctuous and different result.

Using a Chinese bamboo steamer is a wonderful way to cook fish. Scoring the flesh makes it easy to see when it is cooked. The sauce also makes a great accompaniment.

WHOLE THAI-STYLE STEAMED FISH WITH CHILLI, GARLIC & CORIANDER

3 large fresh chillies
(red and/or green)

1 bunch fresh coriander

2 cloves garlic

1 tablespoon finely chopped ginger

2 x one-portion-sized fish,
such as snapper or bream, or 1 large fish

1 tablespoon vegetable oil

1¹/₂ tablespoons sugar

1¹/₂ tablespoons fish sauce (nam pla)

¹/₂ cup (125 ml) chicken or fish stock, or water

1 tablespoon lime or lemon juice

1 teaspoon cornflour

2 fresh red chillies or red capsicum,
cut into fine julienne strips

whole sprigs of coriander

Put the chillies, one coriander root from the bunch, garlic and ginger together in a food processor and blend, or pound together to make a paste.

Trim the fish tails and fins with scissors, wash and pat the fish dry. Score the flesh in three parallel lines on one side. Place in a greased, Chinese bamboo steamer over boiling water. Alternatively, you can place the fish on greased foil and grill, sprinkle with a little lemon juice and white wine and bake in the oven or even fry it.

Heat the oil in a saucepan over a medium to high heat and fry the spice paste, sugar and fish sauce, stirring frequently, until the sugar dissolves and the mixture bubbles. Pour in the stock, stir, bring to the boil and simmer for a few minutes. Stir in the lime or lemon juice. Taste. If necessary add more sugar, fish sauce or lemon or lime juice remembering the classic Thai balance between hot, sour, sweet and salty.

Dissolve the cornflour in a tablespoon of water to make a thin paste. Stir into sauce mixture. Bring back to the boil and simmer for 1 minute until the sauce is clear and slightly thickened.

Place the fish on individual serving plates and pour the sauce over the top. Sprinkle with chopped coriander leaves, julienne of chilli or capsicum and coriander sprigs. Serve with jasmine rice.

Serves 2

PASTA WITH PUMPKIN, HORSERADISH & SILVERBEET

1 butternut pumpkin	1 cup (250 ml) chicken stock
honey	salt and pepper
3 red chillies, seeded and chopped	nutmeg
1 teaspoon horseradish	1/2 bunch silverbeet or spinach
1¼ cups (300 ml) fresh cream	pasta (allow 75 g dry pasta per person)

Peel the butternut pumpkin and cut into chunks. Place in a baking dish and drizzle with honey and roast until done, around an hour. Purée the pumpkin in the food processor, then warm in a saucepan. Add the chillies, a teaspoon or more of horseradish, fresh cream, a cup or so of chicken stock (more if the pumpkin is large), salt, pepper and nutmeg to taste. Roll up some leaves of silverbeet and slice finely to make a chiffonnade. Stir through the sauce and serve over hot pasta.

Serves about 8, depending on the size of the pumpkin

This is an unusual combination that makes a delicious pasta sauce. It is another recipe without specific quantities. Try the above but rely on your taste buds!

SPRING SALMON

A recipe to take advantage of Australia's marvellous salmon. It can be served warm or at room temperature, with the minimum of fuss and is easy to cook, easy to eat and easy to digest.

2 x 160–180 g fillets of salmon or trout

white pepper

1 clove garlic, finely sliced

1¼ cups (300 ml) virgin olive oil, more or less

1 red capsicum, seeded and cut into strips

1 extra clove garlic, very finely sliced

2 fresh mushrooms

¼ bunch shallots

2 tablespoons rice vinegar

½ tablespoon Ketjap Manis (Indonesian sweet soy sauce)

sea salt to taste (optional)

Preheat the oven to the lowest setting, usually around 50°–90°C.

Skin the salmon and season with pepper. Place in an ovenproof dish that just fits the two fish fillets. Sprinkle with slivers of garlic and cover completely with olive oil. Place in the oven for no more than 15 minutes, until the fish is just done and still pink inside.

Using a little of the oil from the fish, sauté the capsicum, additional garlic, mushrooms and shallots until the capsicum is soft but not brown. Remove the salmon fillets from the oil and drain on a paper towel. Add the rice vinegar and Ketjap Manis to the pan. Shake.

Place a piece of salmon on each plate, sprinkle with sea salt to taste and pour over contents of pan. Serve warm or at room temperature. It is best not to refrigerate this dish as this may harden the fish. Accompany with a salad of small leaves such as mizuna, baby endive, etc.

ALTERNATIVE METHOD

To decrease the absorption of oil by the fish, brush the salmon with extra-virgin olive oil, sprinkle with pepper and wrap tightly in foil. Cook in the oven in the same way and proceed as for the previous method.

Serves 2

THAI BEEF SALAD

500 g rump steak (trimmed of fat)
or eye fillet of beef

lettuce

DRESSING

juice of 3–4 limes

1 tablespoon sugar syrup
(or a little more to taste)

2 tablespoons Thai fish sauce (nam pla)

1 red chilli, finely chopped

fresh mint and coriander, chopped

SALAD

cherry tomatoes, halved

Lebanese cucumbers,
finely sliced

Spanish onions,
finely diced

mint leaves

fresh coriander leaves

2 or more (depending on your taste!)
hot chillies, finely chopped

Grill the rump steak if using it or seal the eye fillet well in butter in a frypan. The meat should be rare. Cool and slice it thinly (partially freezing the meat will make it easier).

Combine the ingredients for the dressing and marinate the sliced beef in it.

Mix together all the ingredients for the salad. Serve the beef with lettuce leaves and the salad.

Serves 10 as an entrée, 6 as a main course

An alternative to carpaccio, this is an absolutely up-to-date and extremely economical use of beef. It is also quick to prepare and presents well on the plate. It can be served either as an entrée or with a green salad as a main course.

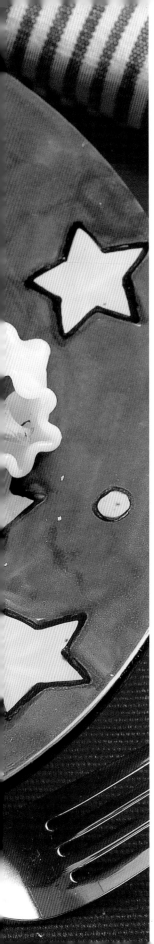

PASTA WITH CHICKEN LIVERS, SAGE & ROCKET

150 g pasta, such as ricciarelle

extra-virgin olive oil

300 g chicken or duck livers

handful of sage leaves

1 bunch rocket or arugula

salt and pepper

Cook the pasta in plenty of salted boiling water.

Get a frypan very hot and pour in some extra-virgin olive oil. Quickly sauté the livers. Add some sage leaves and cook for a few minutes only, so the livers are still pink inside.

Drain the pasta and place in serving bowls. Remove the frypan from the heat. Quickly throw into the pan some rocket, salt, freshly ground black pepper and a little extra olive oil (if there are not many pan juices) and stir lightly. Pour over pasta and serve immediately.

Serves 2

Chicken livers are one of those things you either love or hate. This is a great way to enjoy them if you want to.

CHICKEN BREASTS IN PROSCIUTTO

1 large Granny Smith apple

1 bunch fresh tarragon or dill

6 chicken breast fillets

6 slices prosciutto

SAUCE

1 1/2 cups (375 ml) chicken stock

4/5 cup (200 ml) white wine

2/5 cup (100 ml) cream

Peel, core and slice the apple and cook in a little water until tender. Cool. Chop the tarragon and mix with the apple.

Lay the chicken breast fillets flat and place some apple mixture in the middle of each. Roll up to form a torpedo shape. Place each fillet on a slice of prosciutto and roll this around the chicken to keep it in shape. Lay the rolled chicken breasts on a greased oven tray with the join in the prosciutto against the tray. Bake in a hot oven for 15–20 minutes.

Meanwhile place the sauce ingredients in a saucepan, bring to the boil and reduce until it is thick and bubbly.

Remove the chicken breasts from the oven, cut in half diagonally. Arrange with one half propped on top of the other. Pour over the sauce and serve.

Serves 6

I found that this recipe was always popular when I was a caterer. The beauty of it is that it can be prepared in advance, with only the final cooking to be done before you eat. This makes it ideal for entertaining.

Chicken breasts need good, strong flavours to make them interesting. Red capsicum, especially roasted, makes anything taste good! Made into an aïoli it is particularly delicious.

CHICKEN BREASTS WITH RED CAPSICUM AÏOLI

RED CAPSICUM AÏOLI

1 red capsicum

4 cloves garlic

1–2 egg yolks

salt

1–2 tablespoons
lemon juice

³/₅ cup (150 ml) olive oil

6 chicken breasts

olive oil

12 slices of prosciutto (not too wafer thin)

mixed salad greens

1 punnet cherry tomatoes

Roast or char-grill the red capsicum until black and blistered. Place in a plastic bag while still hot and leave to cool. Peel and remove the seeds.

Make the aïoli by placing the garlic, egg yolks and salt in a blender or food processor and processing to a paste. Add the capsicum and lemon juice and purée. Gradually add the olive oil with the motor running. The slower the olive oil is poured in, the thicker the aïoli will be (it is really a mayonnaise). Taste and adjust seasoning with additional lemon juice, salt and pepper, if required.

Brush the chicken breasts with olive oil and place in a hot cast iron pan with grill markings (or on the barbecue). After 5 minutes or so, turn the chicken breasts over. There should be strong markings on it from the pan. Continue to cook on the other side. When almost done, add the prosciutto to the grill pan or barbecue.

To serve, place a bed of salad greens on each serving plate. Scatter halved cherry tomatoes around the edges. Place a chicken breast in the middle of each plate. Drizzle with red capsicum aïoli and top with two slices of crisp prosciutto.

Serves 6

GREEN CURRY OF CHICKEN

CURRY PASTE

5 green chillies

1 teaspoon black peppercorns

1 onion, chopped

3 cloves garlic

1 stalk lemongrass, sliced finely

1 stalk fresh coriander, chopped

1 teaspoon ground coriander

1 teaspoon cumin

1 teaspoon turmeric

2 teaspoons shrimp paste (kapi)

1kg chicken thigh fillets

butter or oil

2 cans coconut milk

2 extra green chillies

2 extra stalks fresh coriander

2 tablespoons fish sauce (nam pla)

1/2–1 whole bunch basil leaves,
preferably Thai or holy basil

To make the paste, combine the chillies, black peppercorns, onion, garlic, lemongrass, fresh and ground coriander, cumin, turmeric and shrimp paste in a food processor until they form a paste. Use immediately or store in the fridge in a well-sealed jar.

Cut chicken thigh fillets in strips or chunks. Fry the curry paste briefly in a little butter or oil to develop the flavour. Add the coconut milk and stir to combine. Bring to the boil and cook until the mixture thickens and looks oily. Add the chicken, extra chillies and chopped coriander, fish sauce and basil leaves. Simmer for 15 minutes, and it is ready to serve.

Note: By a stalk of coriander, I mean the group of several stems that are attached to the root.

Serves 4–6

For this dish you can either use a good commercial curry paste or make your own.

KANGAROO FILLET WITH RED-CURRANT REDUCTION SAUCE

Don't be afraid of kangaroo. It is a wonderful meat, with all the beneficial properties of red meat, yet very low in cholesterol or fat. It is only tough when overcooked. This is one recipe you should follow to the letter, especially as far as timing is concerned and I promise you will not be disappointed! Your butcher should stock kangaroo meat, otherwise ask for it to be ordered in.

150–180 g kangaroo fillet or strip loin per person

olive oil

2 cups (500 ml) beef stock

1 cup (250 ml) red wine

3–4 good tablespoons red-currant jelly

Brush the kangaroo meat with olive oil and pan fry over a high heat until brown on all sides to seal. Place on a baking tray and put in a hot (200°C) oven for 5 minutes.

Meanwhile pour the remaining ingredients into a frypan and boil at high temperature until they are reduced and thick and syrupy.

Remove the kangaroo from oven, cover with foil and rest for 10 minutes.

To serve, slice the kangaroo and cover with sauce. Serve with a creamy potato dish, such as mashed potatoes or sliced potatoes cooked in the oven with sour cream, and a green vegetable.

PAN-FRIED STEAK WITH TOMATO & OLIVE SAUCE

2 ripe red tomatoes

olive oil

rump steak, enough for four people

2 cloves garlic, chopped

olive pâté (or tapenade)

freshly chopped parsley

Cut a cross into the skin of the tomatoes, then cover them with boiling water for 15–20 seconds. Drain, and you will be able to peel the skin off easily. Cut the tomatoes in half, squeeze out the seeds, then chop coarsely.

Brush a large frypan with olive oil and heat it until very hot. Cook the rump steaks on both sides. When cooked (it will require only a couple of minutes each side if you prefer it rare), remove the steaks and keep them warm.

Add the garlic to the pan and soften for 1 minute. Then add tomatoes and olive pâté, stirring to combine. Bring to a simmer, add some chopped fresh parsley and serve the sauce over the steaks.

Serves 4 with potatoes and a salad

We all enjoy that Aussie staple, steak. This recipe has the advantage of both the steak and the quick-to-make sauce being cooked in the same pan.

LAMB STEAKS WITH ROASTED RED CAPSICUM SAUCE & COUSCOUS

Trim lamb is ideal for a fast meal. Treat it more like chicken or veal, and cook it briefly. Allow three lamb steaks per person, but first prepare the sauce and couscous.

SAUCE

1 red capsicum

salt and pepper

3/4–1 cup (200 ml) chicken or lamb stock (optional)

freshly chopped herbs (optional)

garlic (optional)

18 lamb steaks

olive oil

180 g instant couscous

1/2 cup (125 ml) water or stock

Roast the capsicum in a hot oven for about 20 minutes or until it is black and blistered. Place it immediately in a plastic bag until it is cool enough to handle, then peel it and remove the seeds. Purée the capsicum with salt and pepper. Add some stock if you like – this extends the sauce without any real loss of flavour. Heat it in a saucepan or microwave oven. Chopped herbs or garlic can be added according to taste.

To prepare the couscous, follow the method set out on page 71.

Fry the lamb steaks in a hot frypan with a little olive oil, 2 minutes on each side is plenty. Serve with couscous and the red capsicum sauce.

Serves 6

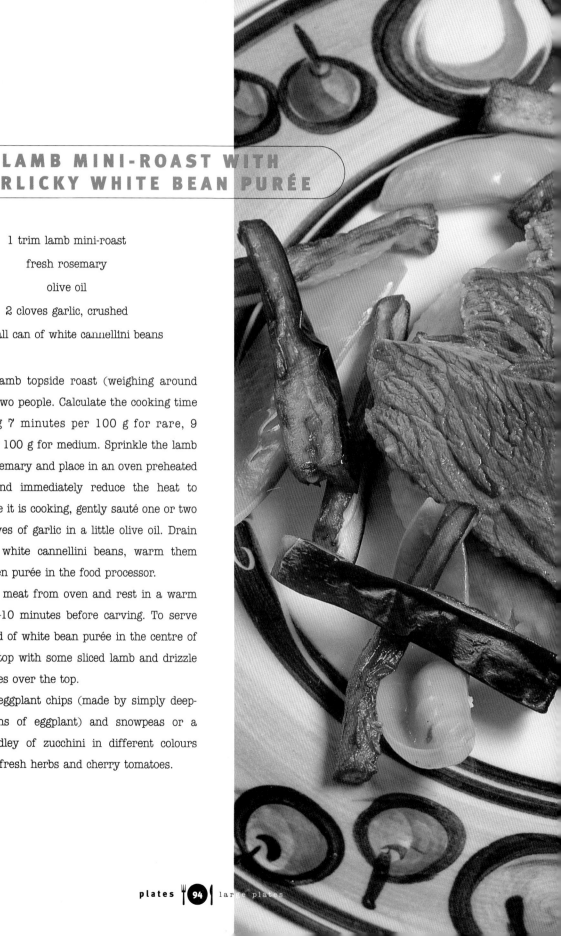

LAMB MINI-ROAST WITH GARLICKY WHITE BEAN PURÉE

1 trim lamb mini-roast

fresh rosemary

olive oil

2 cloves garlic, crushed

1 small can of white cannellini beans

Allow one lamb topside roast (weighing around 400 g) for two people. Calculate the cooking time by allowing 7 minutes per 100 g for rare, 9 minutes per 100 g for medium. Sprinkle the lamb with the rosemary and place in an oven preheated to 220°C and immediately reduce the heat to 200°C. While it is cooking, gently sauté one or two crushed cloves of garlic in a little olive oil. Drain the can of white cannellini beans, warm them through, then purée in the food processor.

Remove the meat from oven and rest in a warm place for 5–10 minutes before carving. To serve put a mound of white bean purée in the centre of each plate, top with some sliced lamb and drizzle the pan juices over the top.

Serve with eggplant chips (made by simply deep-frying batons of eggplant) and snowpeas or a sautéed medley of zucchini in different colours tossed with fresh herbs and cherry tomatoes.

Serves 2

Try this great meal when you are in a hurry. It looks as if it takes much more care and time than it actually does!

BOURBON PORK WITH GLAZED APPLES

Pork fillets are lean but, like chicken, are best enlivened by an interesting sauce. I enjoy the ease of making a sauce in the same pan as the meat is cooked in, especially when it comes to washing up.

1 tablespoon butter	1/2 cup (125 ml) cream
2 apples	1/4 cup (60 ml) stock
2 teaspoons sugar	2 tablespoons bourbon, brandy or calvados
2 pork fillets	salt
2 tablespoons olive oil	freshly ground pepper

Cut the unpeeled apples into eighths, removing the core. Melt the butter in a frypan, add the apples and sprinkle the sugar over. Turn the apples occasionally and cook until tender.

Cut the pork fillets into slices diagonally, make them thin if you wish to cook the pork quickly, thicker for a slightly slower but moister finish. Heat the oil in a separate pan and cook the pork over a high heat, being careful not to overcook it. Remove the meat and pour the remaining ingredients into the pan. Simmer until they have thickened a little and reduced. Adjust the seasoning, if necessary. Pour the sauce over the pork and top with the glazed apples.

Serve with green vegetables in season or a salad.

Serves 3–4 depending on the size of the fillets

sweet plates

BAKED QUINCES WITH ALMOND TUILES

½–1 quince per person

1 teaspoon (5–10 g) butter per quince

2 tablespoons sugar
per quince

250 g mascarpone
or thick cream

ALMOND TUILES

2 egg whites

¼ cup (50 g) vanilla sugar

⅓ cup (50 g) flour

2 tablespoons (50 g) butter, melted

3 tablespoons flaked almonds

Preheat the oven to 200°C. Wash the quinces well. Cut them in half along the core and remove the cores and seeds using a sharp, strong knife. Put each quince half, cut side up, on some foil. Top with a sliver of butter and about 2 tablespoons of sugar per quince (or more to taste, quinces are quite sharp). Wrap up the quinces firmly and place in a baking dish, still with the cut side up. Bake for at least an hour and a half or until tender.

To make the tuiles, combine all ingredients. This mixture can be frozen, but it should be brought back to room temperature before use. Place spoonfuls of the mixture on greased paper or silicone-lined trays, sprinkle with flaked almonds and work into large circles with the back of a spoon.

Cook for a short time at 200°C until golden brown. Remove and drape them immediately over a French-bread tin so that they curl. If the tuiles harden while flat, simply pop them back in the oven to warm so they become pliable again.

Store in an airtight container.

Serve the quince with marscapone or thick cream and the almond tuiles.

Makes lots (12–16 large tuiles)

While this is very fast and easy
to prepare, it does take a while in
the oven, but your patience will
be well rewarded.

HONEYED FIGS

butter

8 figs

4 slices brioche, from a whole loaf

honey

250 g mascarpone or thick cream

The number of figs you will need for this recipe will depend on their size.

Melt enough butter to cover base of the frypan. Slice the figs and sauté them, cut side down, until golden brown, turning them occasionally. Meanwhile butter and toast the slices of brioche. Drizzle honey over the top of the figs and allow it to bubble up. Remove from heat.

Serve figs on or beside the toasted brioche with mascarpone or thick cream.

Serves 4

I'm not sure where this recipe started, but it has become very popular over the last few years. *Vogue Entertaining* published a recipe of Greg Doyle's, but suddenly it seemed to be everywhere. It remains a favourite café item.

STICKY TOFFEE PUDDING

185 g stoned dates

1 cup (250 ml) water

1 level teaspoon
bicarbonate of soda

2 tablespoons (60 g) butter

2 eggs

$^3/_4$ cup (185 g) sugar

1$^1/_4$ cups (185 g) self-raising flour

$^1/_4$ teaspoon vanilla essence

SAUCE

$^7/_8$ cup (150 g) brown sugar

$^2/_3$ cup (150 ml) cream

$^1/_2$ cup (110 g) butter

$^1/_2$ teaspoon vanilla essence

Preheat the oven to 190°C.

To make the pudding, cook the dates in water until they reach a jammy consistency, stirring frequently to break them up. Beat in the remaining ingredients and mix well. Butter and flour an oblong baking tray with edges, and pour in mixture. Bake on the centre shelf of the oven for 25 minutes or until pudding is cooked.

To make the sauce, place all the sauce ingredients in a pan, bring to boil and boil for 5 minutes.

To serve, cut the pudding into wedges and serve with the sauce and thick cream.

Serves 8–10

PLUM CLAFOUTIS

Clafoutis is a traditional French dish that consists of a batter poured over fruit, usually cherries. Plums make a pleasant alternative, and the brandy and flaked almonds give the batter a lift.

750 g plums

1/2 cup (75 g) flour

1/2 cup (110 g) caster sugar

pinch of salt

4 eggs

1 cup (250 ml) milk

2 tablespoons brandy

2 tablespoons
flaked almonds

extra sugar

Preheat the oven to 180°C.

Place the plums in a large saucepan of boiling water. Simmer for 2–3 minutes until just tender. Drain, then plunge into cold water to cool. Cut the plums in half, remove the stems and stones and transfer to a lightly buttered baking dish. If fresh plums are not available, you can use good quality tinned plums – Australian of course!

Place flour, sugar and salt in a bowl or food processor. Beat the eggs in, one at a time, then add half the milk and beat for 5 minutes. Stir in the remaining milk and brandy. Pour mixture over the plums. Sprinkle with flaked almonds. Bake for 40–45 minutes. Sprinkle with extra sugar and serve hot with cream.

VARIATION

Apricots or peaches can be substituted for plums.

Serves 8

Although bread and butter pudding was never difficult to make, this one is incredibly easy. Devised by my food writer colleague, Betty Hinchliffe, there is no need to use sultanas as there is already dried fruit in the fruit loaf.

BREAD & BUTTER PUDDING

butter

1 continental fruit loaf

nutmeg (preferably freshly ground)

4 eggs

2 tablespoons sugar

2 cups (500 ml) milk

1 cup (250 ml) cream

Butter 8-10 slices fruit loaf and place in the bottom of an ovenproof dish that is approximately 30 cm x 20 cm. Sprinkle with nutmeg. Beat the eggs, add the sugar, milk and cream and pour over the bread. Leave for 30 minutes to allow bread to absorb some of the milk mixture.

Heat the oven to 180°C and cook the pudding for approximately 30 minutes or until it is puffed and brown. The flavour will be better if the pudding rests for 5–10 minutes before serving.

Serves 6–8

CRÈME BRÛLÉE

You will be surprised how incredibly quick and easy it is to prepare this classic dish. One that many people love, yet are afraid to make! Traditionally the egg yolks and vanilla sugar are beaten together until light in colour and slightly thickened, then scalded cream is added and the mixture is either whisked over a double boiler or put in a bain-marie in the oven for baking. This version does give less volume, but it is still very good.

1 cup (250 ml) thickened cream

2 egg yolks

$^1/_2$ tablespoon vanilla sugar

caster sugar for glaze

Scald the thickened cream in the microwave – 2 minutes on HIGH should do the trick – in a microwave-safe jug, of course. Then quickly whisk in the egg yolks and vanilla sugar (you can use caster sugar with a couple of drops of pure vanilla essence in it). If you have faith, microwave the mixture on HIGH for 30 seconds, whisk, then microwave on HIGH for another 20 seconds. Don't despair if the mixture bubbles and you think it has curdled, just beat like mad and all will be well. More cautious cooks may care to do this process slowly, using a MEDIUM heat. If you want more volume, but like the convenience of the microwave, beat the eggs together first and then proceed with the microwave method above.

Pour into ramekins and set in the fridge, preferably overnight. Sprinkle the top with caster sugar and a few drops of water to begin the melting process. Caramelise using a blow torch, brûlée iron, or pack the dishes in ice and place briefly under a hot grill. The ice will keep the custard cold.

Serve on its own or with fresh strawberries.

Serves 2–3, depending on the size of the ramekins

POACHED PEACHES WITH GRANITA

Begin this recipe the day before you wish to eat it. Not that it's at all difficult, it just takes time (but no effort!) for the granita to freeze.

1 cup (220 g) sugar

1 cup (250 ml) water

2 cups (500 ml) sparkling wine

4 whole perfect peaches (freestone when in season)

Place sugar, water and sparkling wine in a saucepan and stir to dissolve the sugar. Place the peaches in the syrup and bring to the boil. Simmer for approximately 15 minutes, until the peaches are softened but not mushy. Cool in the liquid.

Remove the peaches and place the liquid in the freezer. Skin the peaches and refrigerate them. Stir the liquid in the freezer occasionally with a fork as it freezes to achieve a granular texture. This is called a granita. You must do this throughout the whole day, the day before you wish to serve the peaches.

To serve, place some granita in a wide-mouthed wine glass. Top with the peach and serve pouring cream separately.

Serves 4

GRATINÉED FRUIT

This recipe includes that old-fashioned favourite, zabaglione. Put it over any seasonal fruit and glaze for an updated approach.

fresh fruit, such as strawberries or mangoes

ZABAGLIONE

2 egg yolks

2–3 tablespoons Marsala

2 tablespoons caster sugar

zest of a lemon

Put all the zabaglione ingredients in the top of a double boiler, you can put them straight in a saucepan if you are careful. Beat them together with a wire whisk over gentle heat until the whole thing has trebled in volume and is light and frothy throughout.

Put the fresh fruit into ramekins and top with the zabaglione. Pop under the griller until brown. Be careful not to burn it.

Serves 4

RHUBARB & STRAWBERRY CRUMBLE

Rhubarb is often overlooked as being rather pedestrian. However, I have fond memories of it from my childhood. Here, combined with strawberries, it is quite grown up.

4 cups peeled and diced rhubarb
(approximately 1 bunch)

1 cup strawberries,
cut in half if large

2 tablespoons (25 g) sugar

1 heaped teaspoon cornflour

CRUMBLE

½ cup (110 g) unsalted butter,
at room temperature

½ cup (165 g) brown sugar

½ cup (75 g) plain flour

½ cup (75 g) quick oats

Preheat the oven to 200°C.

Grease a smallish soufflé or gratinée dish. Place the rhubarb and strawberries in this and lightly mix through the sugar and cornflour. Mix the crumble ingredients together either by hand or in the food processor and place on top. Cook for 25–30 minutes. The juices should bubble up and the top be golden. Serve with thick cream or vanilla ice-cream.

Serves 4

SUMMER PUDDING

1 kg mixed berries, such as strawberries, raspberries, blueberries, boysenberries, youngberries, cranberries, mulberries

¹/₂ cup (110 g) caster sugar

1–2 tablespoons water

12–14 slices day-old white bread

This recipe can either be made as one large pudding or individual ones in small ramekins. Pick over the berries and rinse with water. Cut any large berries, such as strawberries, into smaller pieces. Place in a saucepan with the sugar and water. Simmer for about 5 minutes, stirring occasionally, until the fruit softens, releasing their juice.

Remove the crusts from the bread. If you are making one large pudding, cut one slice into a circular shape to fit the bottom of a 6-cup (1.5-litre) pudding basin. Line the basin or individual ramekins with bread, trimming it so that it fits snugly. There should be some slices left to cover the fruit.

Ladle the fruit and enough juice to moisten the bread into the moulds, reserving a little of the juice. Cover with bread and weight the top with a plate plus something heavy on top. Leave at least overnight, or even for a couple of days.

Shortly before serving, unmould the puddings and baste any white patches of bread with the reserved juice.

I have even frozen this pudding successfully!

Serves 6

Summer pudding is the highlight of British cuisine. It is also one recipe that translates well to our Australian climate.

LEMON OR LIME TART

There are many versions of this delectably zingy tart. Limes are lovely, but if you can't get them, use lemons.

PASTRY

1¹/₄ cups (200 g) plain flour

¹/₂ cup (90 g) icing sugar

3 tablespoons (90 g) unsalted butter, diced

1 egg

1 tablespoon cold water (optional)

FILLING

4 eggs

¹/₃ cup (75 g) caster sugar

1¹/₄ cup (300 ml) cream

juice of 2–3 lemons or limes

icing sugar

For the pastry, put the flour and icing sugar in a food processor and combine for a few seconds. Add the butter and process until the mixture resembles breadcrumbs. Add the egg. Process, stopping as soon as the dough forms into balls and clings around blade. If this doesn't happen, add a little chilled water until it does. Remove, wrap in plastic wrap and refrigerate for at least one hour; the pastry can be left overnight.

Preheat the oven to 200°C.

Roll out the dough on a lightly floured board and line a high-sided flan tin approximately 26 cm across. Press the pastry gently into the tin and use a rolling pin to trim the excess from the perimeter. Prick all over, including the sides, with a fork. Place in the freezer for at least 15 minutes (again, overnight is fine). Cook in the oven for 10–15 minutes until it is golden brown.

Reduce the oven temperature to 170°C.

To make the filling, beat the eggs and caster sugar together until pale. Pour in the cream and, finally, the juice. Pour immediately into the prepared pastry base and bake until it is just set, about 25-30 minutes.

Dredge with icing sugar and serve with whipped or thick cream.

Serves 6–8

YUMMY LEMON PUDDING

An old-fashioned favourite. The top becomes golden brown and cake-like concealing a wonderful lemony sauce underneath.

2 tablespoons soft butter

1/2 cup (110 g) caster sugar

2 tablespoons flour, plain or self-raising
(it doesn't seem to matter!)

juice and zest of 1 large or
1 1/2 smaller lemons

1 cup (250 ml) milk

2 eggs, separated

Preheat the oven to 180°C. Grease an ovenproof dish.

Beat together the butter and sugar until pale and soft. Add the lemon juice and zest, flour, milk and egg yolks and combine well.

Beat the egg whites until stiff and fold into mixture.

Pour into the greased ovenproof dish and bake for 25–30 minutes or until the top is golden.

Serve warm with thick cream.

Serves 4

STONE-FRUIT TART

Adapt this basic recipe to any fruit that is in season. In summer, it's a wonderful opportunity to use peaches and nectarines. At other times of year, use pears or apples.

1 packet filo pastry

3 tablespoon melted butter

2 or 3 peaches or 3 or 4 nectarines

1 tablespoon sugar

Preheat the oven to 200°C.

Have a damp tea towel or cloth ready when working with filo pastry, to prevent it getting brittle.

Unroll the pastry carefully, remove two sheets and brush with butter. Place another two sheets on top and repeat the process until there are ten layers of pastry. (Usually each sheet is brushed with butter, but I find this unnecessary for crisping the filo and leaving it out also reduces the fat content.)

Cut the pastry in half lengthwise and then into six or eight pieces horizontally, so that you end up with twelve or sixteen pieces. This will depend on what size you would like the finished product to be. They can also be cut quite small and served as finger food at the end of a cocktail party.

Peel the peaches carefully (there is no need to peel the nectarines), slice thinly and layer slices on the pastry.

Brush the top with butter, sprinkle with sugar and bake until golden, around 15–18 minutes.

Serves 4–6

Before you make the confit, you will need to poach the pears in wine. Then it is just a matter of boiling and reducing the poaching liquor.

6 firm medium-sized pears,
preferably a little under-ripe

1 cup (220 g) sugar

2¹/₂ cups (600 ml) water

2¹/₂ cups (600 ml) white wine

grated rind 1 lemon (optional)

2 teaspoons
lemon juice (optional)

4 cloves (optional)

1 piece cinnamon stick (optional)

TO POACH THE PEARS

Peel the pears, leaving them whole, and place with remaining ingredients in a saucepan. Ideally the liquid should just cover the pears. If it doesn't, add more water and wine. Simmer gently for up to 20 minutes, until tender. The key to this recipe is slow poaching – do not plunge the pears into boiling liquid and cook quickly or the flavour will not penetrate.

Remove the pears from the liquid, strain the syrup and pour over them. Serve warm or cold.

TO MAKE THE CONFIT

Simply follow the instructions above, omitting the optional ingredients, though perhaps adding a vanilla bean.

After removing the pears, turn up the heat, and boil and reduce the syrup to a caramel consistency. Slice the pears and return to the syrup. Cool. Serve the confit with brie or brioche and mascarpone, or even with ice-cream!

Serves 6

These make a lovely change from larger lemon-curd tarts. This idea was given to me years ago by Jenny Ferguson, who ran a wonderful restaurant in Sydney called 'You and Me' and then wrote a book, *Cooking for You and Me*. It was a favourite.

TINY PASSIONFRUIT BUTTER TARTS

SWEET SHORTCRUST PASTRY

1 cup (125 g) plain flour

1/2 cup (50 g) icing sugar

2 1/2 tablespoons (75 g) unsalted butter, chilled

pinch salt

2 egg yolks or 1 whole egg

1/4 teaspoon vanilla essence

PASSIONFRUIT BUTTER

pulp of 10 passionfruit

1/2 cup (100 g) caster sugar

2 1/2 tablespoons (75 g) unsalted butter

1 whole egg

3 egg yolks

This pastry is very 'short' and quite delicious. However, it is difficult to handle on a hot day because of the high butter content, so try to keep everything cold. Good quality commercial pastry could be substituted but the effort in making it yourself will be well rewarded.

To make the pastry, put the flour, sugar and salt into the bowl of your food processor. Cut the butter into a small dice, then combine briefly using the on/off or pulse switch on your processor. This avoids over-processing, which will toughen the pastry. Add the egg yolks and vanilla essence at the end and process to combine. You may need to add a tablespoon or so of cold water if the mixture does not come together.

Heat the oven to 200°C.

Roll out the pastry and cut with a small crouton or scone cutter. Line tiny tart tins with the pastry and prick it with a fork. Place the tarts in the freezer. When frozen, cook in the hot oven until brown, approximately 10 minutes.

To make the filling, combine all ingredients in a saucepan. Cook gently, stirring all the time until it thickens. Push through a sieve to remove the seeds. Return a few seeds to the mixture, so that it is obvious that it is passionfruit and not just lemon! Store in the fridge.

Dust the tart shells with icing sugar and pipe or spoon in the filling.

Makes lots (at least 24)

HONEY WAFERS WITH CHOCOLATE & MACADAMIA NUTS

200 g unsalted butter, softened

1½ cups (320 g) caster sugar

½ cup (120 ml) honey

1 cup (160 ml) plain flour

4 egg whites

macadamia nuts, chopped

couverture chocolate, chopped

Preheat the oven to 180°C.

Blend together the unsalted butter, caster sugar, honey, flour and egg whites in a food processor until completely smooth.

Spread the mixture thinly on silicone paper in greased and floured baking trays. Sprinkle with toasted, chopped macadamias and chopped couverture or cooking chocolate. Bake in the oven until golden. Cool on the tray, break into pieces and store in an airtight container.

Serves 8

I just love these wafers. I make them for myself or enjoy them at Mesclun, the restaurant in the Crescent on Bayswater Hotel, where chef Anthony Mussarra created them.

basics

MAYONNAISE

It is always worth making your own mayonnaise. This recipe makes it almost as easy as opening a jar anyway!

2 egg yolks or 1 egg yolk and 1 whole egg

1 teaspoon mustard

salt and pepper

2 teaspoons (10 ml) lemon
or lime juice or vinegar

1 cup (200 ml) olive oil

Make mayonnaise by placing the egg yolks, mustard and seasonings in the food processor and blending until creamy. Add 1 teaspoon of juice or vinegar, then slowly drizzle in the olive oil. The more slowly the oil is added, the thicker the mayonnaise will be. Add remaining juice or vinegar. Taste to check the seasoning.

If the mayonnaise should show signs of curdling or breaking, have some boiling water at hand and beat in a tablespoon or so. However, if the mayonnaise still fails to thicken or even begins to curdle, beat another egg yolk in a clean bowl with a teaspoon of vinegar and gradually beat the failed mayonnaise into this.

To make aïoli or garlic mayonnaise, blend one or two garlic cloves with the egg yolks and seasonings.

Serve with crudités or use as the basis for many sauces and dips.

MICROWAVE HOLLANDAISE SAUCE

2 tablespoons (60 g) butter

1–2 tablespoons lemon juice

2 egg yolks

1/4 cup (60 ml) cream

1/2 teaspoon mustard

pepper to taste

Heat the butter on HIGH for 40 seconds in a microwave-safe jug (2-cup size is ideal). Beat in the lemon juice, egg yolks and cream. Cook on MEDIUM for 60-90 seconds. Beat. Repeat if necessary. Add seasoning and beat until smooth.

Makes 3/4 cup

There are certain jobs a microwave simplifies. This method sure beats using a double boiler and a hand whisk!

PESTO

The quantities for this recipe are approximate for there are as many different recipes for pesto as there are cooks. Adapt the amounts given to suit your own taste!

100 g pine nuts

3 cloves garlic

1 bunch fresh basil leaves

pinch salt

3/4 cup (75 g) fresh Parmesan cheese, grated

1/2 cup (100 ml) olive oil

Roast the pine nuts in the oven or cook on HIGH in the microwave for a few minutes until golden brown.

Place the garlic, basil and salt in the food processor and process until they are reduced to a green purée. Add the Parmesan cheese and pine nuts and process to combine with the other ingredients. Then slowly pour in the oil, a little at a time, until the pesto is smooth and well combined.

Pesto can be added to freshly cooked and drained pasta, spread on top of open sandwiches or bruschetta, used to make pesto bread (like garlic bread), stirred into soups or casseroles, poured over boiled potatoes and steamed vegetables or eaten as a dip with breadsticks.

VINAIGRETTE

1 cup (250 ml) olive oil

1 teaspoon sesame oil

1/4 cup (60 ml) balsamic vinegar or tarragon or other flavoured vinegar

1 heaped teaspoon mustard, such as Dijon

1–3 teaspoons sugar syrup

salt and pepper

whole fresh herbs, such as chives, oregano, parsley

1 clove garlic, bruised

Mix the vinaigrette ingredients together by shaking vigorously in a jar. Taste. You may need to adjust to your personal taste by adding a little more oil or vinegar or sugar syrup. Leave the herbs in the jar to flavour the vinaigrette as it matures.

There are as many different vinaigrettes as there are types of oil and vinegar. I give a basic recipe; you can vary it with citrus-fruit juice instead of the vinegar and try it with different flavourings.

BEST-EVER SCONES

I cannot remember how many dozens of these we used to make when my partners and I spent 18 frantic months with Café Cuisine Affaire in Sydney's Northbridge. Certainly our customers just loved them!

4 cups (600 g) self-raising flour

pinch of salt

1¼ cups (300 ml) cream

1¼ cups (300 ml) water

Preheat the oven to 220°C.

Mix the flour and salt in a bowl. Gradually stir in cream and water and mix with your hands to a dough.

Roll out on a floured board and cut with a scone cutter.

Brush the top with milk and place in a hot oven. Cook until brown and done, approximately 15 minutes.

CRISPY FISH BATTER

Fish is coated in batter to keep it moist and tender when frying. The oil should be hot but never smoking, around 190–200°C. Cook only a few pieces at a time and fry until golden. Resting the uncooked fish with the batter on can help it adhere better to the fish.

1 cup (150 g) self-raising flour

pinch salt

1 egg

1 cup (250 ml) beer

Combine the ingredients and dip fish fillets into it before deep frying. The self-raising flour and beer help give a light batter.

SUGAR SYRUP

Sugar syrup is a wonderfully versatile stand-by to keep in the fridge. It can be used in vinaigrettes, to adjust sauces that are too tart, indeed, when-ever some immediate sweetness is required without the problem of having to make sure sugar granules are dissolved.

1 cup (250 g) sugar
1 cup (250 ml) water

Simply bring to the boil together equal quantities of sugar and water, stirring occasionally to dissolve the sugar. Boil for 5 minutes and allow to cool.

BASIC BEEF STOCK

1–2 kg beef or beef and veal bones
2–3 large onions
2 carrots
1 stalk celery (optional)
parsley stalks
1 bay leaf
12 peppercorns
1 cup (250 ml) red wine

Place the bones in a baking tray and roast in a hot oven until they are beginning to brown. Roughly chop the vegetables and add to the baking tray. Rotate the bones and vegetables regularly until they are well browned.
Place bones and vegetables in a large stockpot with the herbs and peppercorns and cover with cold water. Deglaze the baking tray with red wine (or white for chicken stock). As the wine comes to the boil, scrape the tray to release any sediment that has built up. Pour all of this into the stockpot.
Bring to the boil. Simmer for at least 4–6 hours, skimming the surface frequently. Strain, cool and refrigerate the stock overnight. When chilled, it is easy to remove any fat solids that have risen and set on the top.
Use the stock as it is, reduce it to a glaze or freeze for later use.

Adapt this recipe quite simply for other stocks. Just substitute chicken bones for a chicken stock, lamb and veal bones to make lamb stock. The veal bones have a gelatinous quality that enhances the stock.

INDEX

Almond tuiles 100
Apples, glazed, with Bourbon pork 96
Aromatic vegetables 38
Arugula, parmesan cheese and prosciutto salad 26
Asian-scented broth with chicken wontons 54

Baked quinces with almond tuiles 100
Batter, fish 136
Beef, Thai, salad 79
Bourbon pork with glazed apples 96
Bread and butter pudding 108
Bread, with lamb and tomato salsa 60
  muffaletta 22
  vegetable, with herbed olive oil 14
Brioche, mushrooms with 36
Broth with chicken wontons 54

Capsicum, with chicken breast 84
  sauce with lamb and couscous 92
Char-grilled vegetables with olive oil 32
Cheese, sandwiches of eggplant with 28
  arugula and prosciutto salad 26
Chicken breast in prosciutto 82
  breast with red capsicum aïoli 84
  livers, pasta with 80
  salad, Chinese 52
  wontons in Asian-scented broth 54
  green curry of 86
  Hokkien mee noodles 66
Chinese chicken salad 52
Chocolate and macadamia nuts
  with honey wafers 130
Couscous, fish with 70
  lamb steaks with 92
Crab and lemon, spirelli with 58
Crème brûlée 110
Crêpes 34
Crumble, rhubarb and strawberry 116

Devilled prawns 50
Dim sims, pork 20
Duck, Chinese, on rice crackers 10

Easy san choy bau 18
Eggplant, sandwiches 28

Fennel, prawns and 44
Figs in prosciutto 16
  honeyed 102
Fish batter 136
  cakes, Thai 6
  in chermoula marinade and couscous 70
  whole Thai-style 74
Focaccia with lamb and tomato salsa 60
Fruit, baked quinces 100
  gratinéed 114
  honeyed figs 102
  pear confit 126
  poached peaches 112
  tart 124
Granita, with poached peaches 112
Gratinéed fruit 114
Green curry of chicken 86

Herbed olive oil with vegetable bread 14
Hokkien mee noodles 66
Hollandaise sauce 134
Honey wafers with chocolate and macadamia nuts 130
Honeyed figs 102

Kangaroo fillet with red-currant sauce 88
  tail soup 62

Lamb, focaccia and tomato salsa with 60
  mini-roast with white bean purée 94
  with capsicum sauce and couscous 92
Lemon pudding 122
  tart 120
Lime tart 120

Mango and prawn salad 46
Mayonnaise 134
Modern salad Niçoise 68
Muffaletta 22
Mushroom risotto 40
  en brioche 36

Noodles, Hokkien mee 66
Nori rolls with smoked salmon 8
Nuts, macadamia, and honey wafers 130

Olive oil, char-grilled vegetables with 32
  herbed, with vegetable bread 14
Oysters with different toppings 4

Pan-fried steak with tomato and olive sauce 90
Passionfruit butter tarts 128
Pasta, penne alla Napolitana 41
  spaghetti with prosciutto and rocket 56
  spirelli with crab and lemon 58
  with chicken livers, sage and rocket 80
  with pumpkin, horseradish and silverbeet 76
Peaches, poached, and granita 112
Pear confit 126
Penne alla Napolitana 41
Pesto 135
Plum clafoutis 106
Poached peaches and granita 112
Pork, Bourbon, with glazed apples 96
  dim sims 20
  easy san choy bau 18
Potato roesti with smoked salmon 2
Prawns and fennel 44
  and mango salad 46
  devilled 50
  spicy Thai 42
Prosciutto, arugula and cheese salad 26
  chicken breast in 82
  spaghetti with 56
  with figs 16
Pudding, bread and butter 108
  plum clafoutis 106
  sticky toffee 104
  summer 118
  yummy lemon 122
Pumpkin, horseradish and silverbeet. pasta with 76

Quinces, baked, with almond tuiles 100

Ravioli, seafood 48
Rhubarb and strawberry crumble 116
Rice crackers with Chinese duck 10
Risotto, mushroom 40
Salad, arugula, cheese and prosciutto 26
  Chinese chicken 52
  Niçoise, modern 68
  prawn and mango 46
  spring vegetable 30
  Thai beef 79
Salmon, smoked, and nori rolls 8
  smoked, crêpe cake 34
  smoked, with potato roesti 2
  spring 78
San choy bau 18
Sandwiches of eggplant, tomato and goat's cheese 28
Sauce, garlic cream 44
  hollandaise 134
  mayonnaise 134
  pesto 134
  red capsicum 92
  red capsicum aïoli 84
  red-currant reduction 88
  sweet chilli 46
  tomato 60
  tomato and olive 90
Scones 136
Seafood ravioli 48
Soup, kangaroo tail 62
Spaghetti with prosciutto and rocket 56
Spicy Thai prawns 42
Spirelli pasta with crab and lemon 58
Spring salmon 78
  vegetable salad 30
Steak, pan-fried 90
Stone fruit tart 124
Stuffed zucchini flowers 12
Sugar syrup 137
Summer pudding 118
Syrup, sugar 137

Tart, lemon or lime 120
  stone fruit 124
  tiny passionfruit butter 128
Thai beef salad 79
  fish cakes 6
Tiny passionfruit butter tarts 128
Toffee pudding, sticky 104
Tomato and olive sauce, steak with 90
  penne alla Napolitana 41
Tuna modern salad Niçoise 68
  wasabi and fresh herb butter, with 72

Vegetables, aromatic 38
  char-grilled, with olive oil 32
  pasta with 76
  spring, salad 30
Vinaigrette 135

Whole Thai-style fish with chilli, garlic and coriander 74

Yummy lemon pudding 122

Zucchini, stuffed flowers of 12